What the Trumpet Taught Me

What the Trumpet Taught Me
Kim Moore

smith|doorstop

the poetry business

Published by The Poetry Business
Campo House,
54 Campo Lane,
Sheffield S1 2EG
www.poetrybusiness.co.uk

Text copyright © Kim Moore 2022
Cover artwork and illustration copyright © Emma Burleigh 2022
The moral rights of the author have been asserted.

All rights reserved.
Without limiting the rights under copyright reserved above,
no part of this publication may be reproduced, stored in
or introduced into a retrieval system, or transmitted, in any form or by any
means (electronic, mechanical, photocopying, recording or otherwise),
without the prior written permission of both the copyright owner
and the above publisher of this book.

Designed & typeset by The Poetry Business.
Cover Image by Emma Burleigh.
British Library Cataloguing-in-Publication Data.
A catalogue record for this book is available
from the British Library.

Smith|Doorstop is a member of Inpress
www.inpressbooks.co.uk.
Distributed by IPS UK, 1 Deltic Avenue,
Rooksley, Milton Keynes MK13 8LD.

ISBN 978-1-914914-14-0
eBook ISBN 978-1-914914-15-7

The Poetry Business gratefully acknowledges the support
of Arts Council England.

I get along without you very well
Of course I do
Except perhaps in spring
But I should never think of spring
For that would surely break my heart in two

> 'I Get Along Without You Very Well',
> Hoagy Carmichael

O trumpeter, methinks I am myself the instrument thou playest,
Thou melt'st my heart, my brain – thou movest, drawest,
changest them at will ...

> 'The Mystic Trumpeter', Walt Whitman

For my twin sister, Jody

I'M TEN YEARS OLD when my teacher asks the class who would like to play a brass instrument. Because I'm the sort of child who volunteers for everything, my hand shoots into the air. And though I believe I'm never chosen, this time my teacher picks me, along with my twin sister and two other children in the class. I don't even know what a brass instrument is, but I know I want to be chosen.

In our school, everyone knows what recorders and violins are. We have a school orchestra, led by a teacher called Mrs M. If you show promise on the recorder, eventually Mrs M invites you to change to the violin. Mrs M writes letters above the musical notes for the recorders, but the violin players have to learn to read music. When she offers me the violin, I refuse. I know the violin sounds terrible. I blame the instrument rather than the children wielding the bow.

Mrs M has short dark hair and huge spectacles. She writes out parts so we can accompany the whole school in hymn practice. Every morning we line up in front of the piano to practise together. Mrs M's voice is harsh and nasal. She can cut through twenty squeaking recorders and out-of-tune violins without even standing up from her piano stool. We play as the rest of the school sing along, using books held together with tape along the spines. Hymns like 'When A Knight Won His Spurs' – my favourite because the words feel like a poem, or 'He's Got The Whole World In His Hands', which I hated because it was repetitive and dull.

THERE'S A PHOTOGRAPH of me and my twin sister, taken the first day we brought a brass instrument home. I'm standing and holding a euphonium that's clearly too big for me. I think this must have belonged to our school – probably an instrument found in the back of a cupboard and forgotten about.

I'm balancing on one leg, with my other foot on the sofa and supporting the euphonium with my knee. My sister is sitting down, looking grumpy, her leg stretched out and her foot about to kick me, or perhaps push me away. She was probably angry at having to share, having to wait, something that as twins we were always forced to do, and resented deeply. I look happy and pleased with myself – I'm smiling around the large mouthpiece, peering from behind the bell, although I can't remember any of this. If it wasn't for the photo, I wouldn't even know I'd ever taken a euphonium home, that any of this happened.

Although writing this now, I suddenly start to doubt whether it was me holding the instrument at all. Maybe it was my sister, and I was the one doing the kicking, disgruntled and irritated by her happiness. I haven't seen the photo for years – I don't even know if it exists in its physical form so I can't check the truth, and my sister doesn't remember anything about the moment it was taken.

My parents take us to a brass band, recommended by my new brass teacher, Mr P, as a place we can get an instrument for free. I ask for a cornet, after watching a young girl playing one with a pearl-like sheen. My sister is given a tenor horn. The conductor, who says we can call him by his first name, W, tells us to join in with the rehearsal, though we cannot read music. I'm told to sit next to a girl with a fox-like face.

I don't understand why the music in front of me has numbers above each note, rather than letters. I don't understand that the numbers correspond to the valves I should be pressing down. I don't even know they are called valves. I'm happily playing along, pressing the valves whenever I feel like it. I don't know a conductor can hear one person playing a wrong note, even when there are thirty other people playing. Eventually, when I find this out, it seems as if it's a

superpower, and one I'll never possess.

W is an elderly man with bone-white hair. He waves his arms, urging us onward. Although it doesn't seem as if anybody is looking at him, or noticing what he's doing, I understand he is important, that the weather of the room starts and finishes with him.

I STAY BEHIND after junior band rehearsal to listen to the senior band. They play the theme tune to *Rocky*. I don't know it's the theme tune to *Rocky*. I think it's the most profound and beautiful thing I've ever heard. I have goosebumps on my arms, although it's not the staccato fanfare of the cornets at the beginning, but the entrance of the lower brass that makes my heart lurch. At some point in the piece, it feels like the music 'turns'. It's at this point I understand what yearning means, although I don't have a name for it, this feeling, this longing. Later, I understand this was a key change. But this is 1992. I'm eleven years old and falling in love.

The oldest trumpets in the world were discovered in King Tutankhamun's tomb in 1922 by British archaeologist Howard Carter. One of the trumpets was made of silver, the other of bronze. When they were found, they'd not been played for 3000 years.

I imagine picking the silver trumpet up, how light it would be, like a hollow branch. I imagine balancing the weight of it in my hand, of the journey towards the mouth, of filling it with breath for the first time in centuries.

I'm thirteen years old. We're being forced to march up and down in the local park by our new band conductor, R, who is wearing a bass drum, pounding it louder and louder to try and keep us all in time. Our left feet must hit the floor on the first and third beat of the bar.

R tells us to mime, says he doesn't trust us not to fall over. Even the percussionist is only allowed to carry his drumsticks. I imagine someone from school seeing this and wonder if it's possible to die of embarrassment.

Some people miss W, the old conductor, who waited patiently for us to finish chatting between each piece we played. With W, we didn't really rehearse, just played through piece after piece from beginning to end. W used to give us a break halfway through rehearsal, and we would go outside and play British bulldog in the car park.

One evening R came in to listen to our rehearsal. He was the senior band conductor and had never shown any interest in the junior band before. That night it was raining, so at breaktime we stayed inside, running around the hall, leaping over our instruments, shoving chairs around and yelling at each other. R stood and watched silently from a corner of the band room, his arms crossed. At the end of the break, we all took our seats, giddy and sweaty from running around. R came to the conductor's stand and began to shout at us for our recklessness. We'd left our instruments on the floor, not even putting them away in their cases.

W walked out halfway through our telling-off and never returned. I liked W, but I don't remember asking where he went or whether he was coming back. R took over and began conducting, dissecting what we were playing, asking each section to play certain parts by themselves, every now and then picking out individual players for praise. Nobody said a word for the rest of that rehearsal, apart from R. Even our parents sat around the edge of the room in shame-faced silence.

IN REHEARSALS, R jumps up and down in frustration if we miss a key change. He throws the baton across the room if we make the same mistake repeatedly, shouts at people if they haven't practised, yells if we don't observe the dynamics and roars wordlessly if we slow down or speed up without being directed. I think he's wonderful. He never shouts at me, but then I practise for an hour every day, sitting at the dining table with my twin sister, propping our music on our cases because we don't have our own music stands.

We play through the pieces in our band folders. Mine has 'Solo Cornet' embossed in gold on the front. Hers has '1st Horn'. But the folder I really want is 'Principal Cornet' and the folder she really wants is 'Solo Horn'. To be promoted to 'Principal Cornet' or 'Solo Horn' you have to prove you're better than the person who is already sitting there.

To make a sound on a brass instrument, you must put your lips together and make them vibrate. Although you may think I've just explained this in language, I haven't really. It's better just to watch someone do it, and then copy without thinking.

IN 1939, BRITISH BANDSMAN James Tappern was chosen to play the trumpets found in King Tutankhamun's tomb live on BBC radio. In the recording he blows three notes. I can hear how he's riding each one, straining to keep control of it, to find his way around the instrument.

Of course, that's not the whole story. The first attempt to play the trumpets ended in disaster. A bandsman from the Egyptian Army was originally chosen for the task, and valiantly tried to wring more than a single pitch from the silver trumpet, with no success. He then decided to use a modern bugle mouthpiece. The stories of what happened next vary, but I'm shocked when I read one account, that the nameless bandsman, because the bugle mouthpiece did not fit properly, smacked it with the palm of his hand further into the trumpet. The silver trumpet shattered into fragments, and the bandsman was left holding only the stem.

Alfred Lucas, a member of Howard Carter's archaeological team was hospitalised with shock. Even more extraordinarily, King Farouk, the King of Egypt, happened to be touring the Cairo Museum and entered the room just as the trumpet shattered. The king then got down on his hands and knees to help gather up the precious shards of silver.

IT'S SUMMER, nearly the end of term and our walk back from school has left both of us sweaty and bad-tempered. We decide we're not going to practise today. Instead of getting our instruments out straight away, we go and sit in the backyard, sunbathing and eating ice lollies from the freezer.

My dad pulls up in his work van and walks through the house and into the garden. He's covered in dust from the building site. He asks us why we're not practising. We reply that we didn't feel like it today, that it was too nice to sit inside. He says nothing, just turns around and goes back into the house. We sense something is wrong and follow him inside. He says that as we can't be bothered to play, for just one hour out of the whole day, he will return the instruments back to the band, to be used by children who will appreciate them and not waste our conductor's time. We're sobbing by this point, promising we'll never miss practising again, hanging onto his arm as he tries to leave. He hovers at the door, undecided, before relenting and passing the cases back to us. We make our way to the dining table, our faces red and blotchy with crying.

I'm fourteen and on a camping holiday with the brass band, somewhere in Wales. Halfway through the week, our conductor decides to set up a rehearsal in the middle of the campsite.

Afterwards we all go down to the children's playground, despite being too old to be in there. The trombone player climbs into a baby swing and we push her higher and higher. Eventually we get bored of this, and she tries to get out, but she's stuck. We attempt to pull her out, but it's no good. She's completely wedged in.

We run to get help. I'm proud that it's my father who has a toolkit in the car, who unscrews the seat, dismantling it completely so that she can escape.

AND EVERY YEAR, playing hymns in Victoria Park at the cenotaph. Learning the Last Post by heart. Standing in band uniform, and no extra coats allowed, and just thin black shoes, and the girls must wear skirts, and no woolly hats when you play, it's not part of the uniform, though gloves (black) are allowed. Rock on your heels if your feet are tired, or cold. Don't look bored. The rhythm of the service running through you. Not just the hymns, the cannon firing and the birds scattering into the sky, but also the words. *They shall not grow old as we who are left grow old.* November circling around again, and always grey, and always cold, and thinking *you'll be part of this, every year of your life.* The open fifth. The call unanswered.

AND EVERY YEAR in December, playing Christmas carols under lampposts. Learning each carol by heart so I don't need to take my gloves off to turn the page. Falling in love with my own sound on an empty street. Noticing vibrato for the first time, but never asking what it is, only taking it in, letting it into my body.

We stand in a circle to play, shoulder to shoulder. Our parents go from house to house with collection tins. Sometimes I turn away and play into the darkness, into the night. Sometimes it's icy and we must walk carefully. The instrument protected at all costs. I fall over and manage to keep my cornet held aloft in the air. Everybody cheers.

THE LEGEND is that King Tutankhamun's trumpets call conflict into being, that they are cursed.

As evidence: the start of World War II only a few months after they were first played, live on the BBC from Cairo.

See also: the sounding of the silver trumpet just prior to the Six Day War between Egypt and Israel in 1967.

See also: the Gulf War, which broke out in 1990, shortly after the silver trumpet was blown.

See also: the silver trumpet, blown in 2011 and followed swiftly by the Egyptian Revolution.

I REMEMBER A MAN in the senior band accidentally sitting on his cornet, but I don't remember who. I remember it happening at the worst possible time, maybe just before we were due to go on stage at a concert or contest, but I can't swear to this. I remember it being completely flattened, like a thin sheet of silver paper, though now I think this can't be true. Maybe the horror I felt back then has created that image in my mind in the intervening years – surely nobody could squash a cornet so decisively with just the weight of their body.

And I remember an Eb bass player deciding to leave his bass near a radiator to warm up, rather than having to blow air through it himself, and I'm sure, as sure as I can be, that this was before a contest, and that when he started to play, he was horribly out of tune, parts of the instrument warm and parts of it freezing cold.

I remember R being furious about this, so

angry that he couldn't speak or bring himself to look at any of us afterwards, as if we were all culpable.

My dad is transposing a duet so my sister and I can play together – me on my cornet, her on the tenor horn. He's counting ledger lines, transposing by numbers because he never learnt to read music. He's writing the parts out carefully by hand, first with pencil and then he'll go over them with a black pen.

I'll be careless with these parts. I'll crease them, rip them by mistake, make them unreadable in various ways and ask him to write them out again. Or my sister will leave them somewhere or lend them to somebody and forget who, or not bother to ask for their return.

My dad's leaning on a road atlas, using a ruler with *Scaffold Services* written across it. He's making sure the stem of every note is straight, ensuring none of the bar lines lean one way or the other.

ONCE UPON A TIME a girl and a man walked for two days in the wild. The man was a kind of teacher and had known the girl since she was ten, but she also thought of him as a friend, also thought of him as a kind of other-father.

The man bought a cheap second-hand trumpet. He said he wanted to learn, but really he bought it because he loved to hear the girl play, and he wanted her to play for him. The girl would not bring her precious cornet into the wild, and so the man bought his trumpet, not understanding the world of difference between the two instruments.

The man carried the trumpet for many miles in the wild, up and down hills, through bogs and streams and across stepping stones and bridges. The trumpet was wedged in his rucksack without a case, the mouthpiece and the leadpipe thrusting upwards from the opening of the bag, at a slight slant to the sky.

The man and the girl talked about poetry and music and university and language and not just what she wanted to be when she was older but who she wanted to be. They talked for hours as they walked and didn't notice that the sun had slipped away from the world and that dusk had arrived.

In the distance, lights from a far-away farmhouse blinked into existence. The man began unpacking the tent and handed the girl the trumpet. He told her to play something, anything. 'Play something Spanish,' he said and at first the girl protested. She was shy, nervous, worrying they would get in trouble somehow for making a noise in such a quiet place, but eventually she lifted the trumpet to her mouth and called across the hills. At the first note, farm-dogs started to bark and more lights came on in the distance. The man laughed and the girl smiled as they imagined the people, safe and warm in their houses, and what they might think of the strange sound floating in on the wind.

Eventually the girl changed into a woman, and so the man tried to change from a teacher-father-friend into a man and then something inside the girl was broken, or if not broken, made still, or if not made still, left in shadow, never to be looked at again, or spoken of, or thought of, or acknowledged.

Despite this, she remembers that night with great love – the hill, and the blue-grey quality of the dusk, and the sound of the trumpet going out into good clean air and the dogs barking, and the wild echoes. She will remember it her whole life, the light and the darkness, the sound and the silence.

Those wild echoes – here they are, ringing through Alfred Lord Tennyson's poem 'The Splendour Falls On Castle Walls'.

Blow, bugle, blow, set the wild echoes flying,
Blow, bugle; answer, echoes, dying, dying, dying.

I cannot read those lines without singing them in my head, hearing them through the music of Benjamin Britten's *Serenade for Tenor, Horn and Strings*. I hear the French horn answer the singer, leaping from note to note, pretending to be a bugle. I hear the word *dying* repeated three times before it's changed from word to sound, from meaning something to enacting something. The word dying dies away. I see a young girl, almost a woman, standing on a hill in the gathering dusk, bringing a trumpet to her lips.

I'm sixteen and taking A-Level music, which means lessons with a new teacher, Mr B, who convinces me to try the trumpet. He tells me that with the cornet, I'm limited to playing in brass bands. With the trumpet, I can do anything – orchestras, pit bands, soul bands, big bands, jazz bands. He lends me his old trumpet, and I hardly touch my cornet after this, only using it when I go to brass band rehearsal twice a week.

I start to feel embarrassed by my cornet case. Although I didn't know it till now, it's the case of a child – covered in stickers from cereal boxes that loudly proclaim words like 'RAD' and 'GRRREAT' in fluorescent colours.

My new trumpet teacher has long hair that he ties back in a ponytail. He rides a motorbike. He gives me my first paid gig – the second trumpet chair in a week-long performance of *Singing In The Rain* at the Haymarket Theatre in Leicester.

The orchestra pit smells of a mix of aftershave and stale air and the sudden darkness sends a jolt of excitement running through me. The ceiling of the pit is the floor of the stage, and it groans and creaks throughout the performance. All the men in the orchestra are dressed in tuxedos, whilst the few women wear long black dresses. It's strange to see my trumpet teacher, usually dishevelled and in jeans and a T-shirt, with his hair scraped back neatly.

I'm paid £150 for the week. It's 1998 and it feels like a fortune.

EVERY SATURDAY I work from 9–5 in a gift shop in the town centre. For this full day's work, with half an hour for lunch, I earn a total of £23. To be fair to the owner, my boss, I don't do very much to earn even this miniscule amount. I sit behind the till and take money from the odd customer that wanders in, always with the owner hovering nearby to supervise. Sometimes I'm set loose with the ticket gun and allowed to label individual items on the shelves.

Every Saturday in the giftshop, my boss puts Madonna's *Ray of Light* album on repeat, all day. One day I suggest a different album. He looks at me as if I've just said something incomprehensible. I train myself to shut background music out and this skill lasts my whole life and is useful in more ways than I could have ever predicted – though even now I shudder if a song from that album comes on the radio.

My parents think it's a good idea I have a job and that it's perfectly reasonable to stand all day on your feet in a gift shop, being bored for £23. They tell me this is What Work Is. But I'm not sure this is true. Or at least it's only one truth. I have the £150 from playing in *Singing in the Rain* in cash in my pocket. It's more money than I've ever seen. I realise work sometimes doesn't have to feel like work.

I'M SEVENTEEN and in my second year of A-Levels, performing regularly now with my trumpet teacher. I can sight-read anything put in front of me. My teacher jokingly says if I can't play something the first time, I'll never play it, and I know it's almost true.

My A-Level music teacher tells me I'm not good enough to go to music college. I don't tell my parents or my trumpet teacher that she said this.

I know she doesn't like me and doesn't know what to do with me or my twin sister, that she can't believe we've never been to an orchestral concert or visited an art gallery. She doesn't understand why we've never sung in a choir, why my instrument doesn't belong to me. She doesn't understand brass bands and says the brass band is a Waste Of Time. I don't tell my parents that either.

SHAKESPEARE WROTE, 'Sound trumpets! Let our bloody colours wave! And either victory, or else a grave', which is really the same as my trumpet teacher's advice, given before each show: 'If in doubt, blast it out.'

I'm eighteen and I've just been accepted into music college. Not one of the best in the UK, but still a music college. I'm still playing on a borrowed trumpet from my teacher, still saving up my £23 a week to buy my own, but it's taking too long.

I've less than a year to save up enough money to buy my own trumpet. I draw a trumpet across four pages that I tape carefully together. I divide the trumpet into 1800 small squares, which is what a Vincent Bach Stradivarius with a 43-inch bell and reverse tuning slide will cost. There's no question of asking my mum and dad for the money. I know they can't afford it.

I get a new job, selling double glazing over the phone. My A-level teacher says I should be spending my time practising and studying, not working 'dead-end jobs'. I don't tell her that most of my family do jobs like this – in factories, on scaffolding sites, plastering walls or cutting hair, serving dinners in junior schools or caring for the elderly in the daytime and then supplementing their wages with bar work in the evening.

At my new job, every time I make an appointment over the phone for a salesman to call round and give a quote for new doors or windows, I get an extra £10 on top of my hourly minimum wage rate. If I make three appointments in one week, I get a £100 bonus. If the salesman sells anything, I get 10% of the total for making the appointment. In my first week I earn £800.

Every time I earn any money, I colour in the little squares. I'm in a race against time – I have to earn enough money to buy a trumpet before I leave for university so I can give my teacher his instrument back. But I'm also in a race against my teacher's trumpet, which is slowly falling apart. Both water keys are held together by elastic bands, and every now and again they come loose. The valves are temperamental and often stick, no matter how much I clean them, but more worryingly, the metal is thin in places, as thin as paper. I could make a hole in it with a finger if I tried.

THERE ARE FOUR HUNDRED and sixty-five steps to make a Bach Stradivarius trumpet, and each trumpet contains one hundred and twenty separate parts. Strad trumpets come in five different bore sizes – the bore being the inside diameter of the tubing. The difference between the medium and large bore trumpet is the width of a human hair, and this tiny variation can radically alter tone, resistance and air flow.

You can watch much of the process of making a Bach Stradivarius trumpet online. In one video, a bell specialist takes a single piece of metal and brings the two edges together and seals them using various tools – what looks like a wooden paddle, then a wooden hammer, then a metal hammer, and then fire.

In the video, there are shots of trumpet bells gathered together in containers. They look like strange flowers – the flared ends ripple in waves rather than forming a perfect circle at this point. To create the recognisable, circular trumpet bell, each one is placed on a mandrel and hammered into shape. A wire is inserted around the edge of the bell to strengthen it, and then the metal is folded back over itself to create the rim.

To make the curve in the bell, which will eventually connect to the valves, the bell is filled with soapy water and frozen in liquid nitrogen. Once the water inside is frozen, the bell specialist folds it using a bending jig. The ice in the bell provides counter pressure whilst the soap in the ice means that it stays pliable as the metal is manipulated. In the videos of this process, the bend in the metal is created so easily, it's as if it's not metal at all, as if each bell has not come through fire and ice and survived.

AT MUSIC COLLEGE, I fall in love with a man because of the way he dances, which is like a cross between Mick Jagger and Liam Gallagher. But that's not entirely true. That makes me want to have sex with him. What makes me fall in love with him is my lecturer telling all of the first-year music students that this boy, this man *is the only musician in this place who knows his scales*.

I cannot imagine or understand that girl, that young woman now.

I LOSE THE TRUMPET I saved up for and I never see it again.

You could say this happened because of the man who danced like Mick Jagger. We leave his house together in the morning and catch a bus into town. The trumpet is with me when I leave, and then suddenly disappears. You could say this happened because I was hungover or because I was tired. You could say I lost the trumpet because I was in love, because I was concentrating only on him, because I was not really there on the bus with the man who danced like Mick Jagger, the trumpet perched where? Between my legs? In the luggage space? I can't remember. I was already moving into our future, into the moment of parting, walking backwards. I was young. I couldn't take my eyes from him.

I claim on my insurance and get another trumpet, exactly the same as the first, a shadow brother of the one I saved up for.

During the Egyptian riots and looting of 2011, the bronze trumpet from King Tutankhamun's tomb was stolen, along with fifty-three other objects from the museum. Miraculously, the bronze trumpet was found a few weeks later in a black bag on a chair in the Shubra Metro station. Inside the bag were other looted items from the museum – a gilded wooden statue of the boy king, a funerary figurine or ushabti and a piece of Tutankhamun's fan.

It's thought that the thief became afraid after the curator of the museum intimated in *Ahram Online* that the trumpet was cursed. The widely accepted theory seems to be that the thief deliberately left their loot somewhere it would be found and returned.

I'm not so sure. Maybe the thief was distracted by their lover, or thoughts of their lover. Maybe they were trying to work out whether it was possible for them to carry on as the least-loved one, as the one that would be left behind. Maybe this is what made them put the bag down on a chair and leave it there. The train pulled up to the platform. Their lover was standing, impatient and ready to board. The thief stood up to follow and didn't look back, didn't realise they'd left the bag until later, much later.

Or maybe their lover loved them as much as they were loved and urged the thief to leave the bag of war and sadness behind, to not bring it into their home. Maybe they both looked through the window of the train at the black bag, abandoned on the chair. Maybe they turned and kissed each other, or held each other's hands, or looked into each other's eyes and quickly forgot about the world, about money, about a bronze trumpet waiting to be found.

At music college, I practise every day for three hours, but I'm practising the wrong things. I'm obsessed with what can be measured, like double tonguing, triple tonguing, like being able to play Arban's 'Carnival of Venice' or flying up and down every scale exercise I can find. All of this is the cornet repertoire I was brought up on, the pieces I loved, but I'm playing them on the trumpet.

I know what I want – to make a living playing my trumpet – but I have no idea how to get there.

I need my A-Level teacher with the cruel face and short blonde bob to tell me I'm practising the wrong things. I need her to admit she was wrong, because here I am, at music college, but I need to admit she was also right, because there's nothing in me good enough to become a solo trumpet player.

I should be practising orchestral excerpts, I should be going to orchestral concerts, I should be practising transposition and having lessons from trumpet players who perform in theatres and orchestras. I should be asking for a chance to dep. But I'm twenty years away from knowing these things.

I join an ex-army wind band called The Yorkshire Volunteers. One of my lecturers at music college is the conductor, so there are a few students who attend. The band was 'disbanded' in the 1998 Strategic Defence Review, but retained the right to wear the Queen's uniform in public and to run itself as an army band, albeit one populated by civilians.

I don't understand the significance of any of this at the time, but it's embedded in the ethos of the band. I learn how to polish shoes, how to perform more complicated marching manoeuvres – figures of eight, spirals. I learn to dress (align with the person to the side), to cover (align with the person in front). I learn the speed of the Quick March, which is 120 beats a minute, and the Slow March, which is 60 beats a minute. I know these speeds in my body. I know how they feel in my blood, in my breathing. I'll know them all my life.

I listen for the double tap from the drum major, which tells us something is about to happen, like stopping at the next double bar, or turning in another direction, or changing music, or getting ready. This band feel like my family, all over again.

I DON'T MISS MY OLD LIFE whilst I'm at music college. I'm beginning a pattern I'll repeat over and over of travelling light, of moving to a new place and taking nothing of the old with me, of forgetting the people I leave behind.

Arthur Lane was a British army bugler captured by the Japanese during the fall of Singapore in 1942. He worked on the notorious Burma Railway and played the Last Post every time a prisoner-of-war died, whatever their nationality. He became known as the musician of the dead.

He kept a meticulous note of the names of the dead on a roll of army-issue toilet paper, despite a penalty of death for any prisoner carrying written material. At the end of his three and a half years as a prisoner of war, he'd played the Last Post over 3000 times. When he returned home he never played the Last Post again.

THERE'S A VIDEO ONLINE of a masterclass, taking place at the Royal Northern College of Music in Manchester with Håkan Hardenberger and a student, Elizabeth Fitzpatrick. She's playing Bohuslav Martinů's *Sonatine for Trumpet and Piano*.

At one point during the masterclass, Hardenberger says, 'most people don't listen and then you start to tell them to listen to themselves and then they start to listen after they played but real listening is listen before'.

Of course I knew, before watching this video, that there are no notes in the trumpet other than the ones you put there yourself. I knew that every note must sound first in your mind, otherwise – disaster. But I only knew this thought in my body. I'd never heard it spoken out loud. Hardenberger goes on to say that the trumpet, after all, is 'just a bit of plumbing'.

I can tell the student, Elizabeth, is nervous.

You can see it in her body, the way she holds herself as he sings along whilst she's playing. Her smile seems to want to both placate and acknowledge what Hardenberger means when he says 'no, no, that made me uncomfortable' in response to the way she plays a phrase. Her eyes drop when he says 'no, no, don't do the little chickens' – referring to how she's stopping the notes with her tongue, rather than interrupting the air with it.

When he plays the phrases in question back to her, his sound is like honey compared to water, rich and effortless and something not quite human about it. I can hear the breath in her sound, the anxiety. It feels as if I can hear all the vulnerability that is poured into girls, but his sound is pure music, pure song.

The next masterclass is with another student, Nick Wright. He isn't any better a player than Elizabeth, and I think he's just as nervous, but there's something else that I'm finding difficult to articulate that's in the room when Elizabeth is playing. In *Gendering Poetry*, Vicki Bertram writes that women poets have to 'confront the implications of being a female on public display, with the connotations of sexual objectification, in a context that traditionally disregards the body'.

This is just as true for female musicians I think, particularly female brass players. It's only in my lifetime that women have finally been allowed to play in the top brass bands in the country. Is it that Elizabeth is a 'female on public display' – that somehow she must negotiate that, before she thinks about breathing, or using her tongue to interrupt the air instead of stopping it; is it this that stands between the note she hears in her mind and the one that comes out of the trumpet; is it this that stands between her and Hardenberger, that makes all of this so awkward?

To a non-musician, this might seem like torture – to have a lesson not just in front of a live audience, but recorded and made public, to take part in a masterclass where it's easy for everyone to hear the difference in tone and technique between you and one of the greatest contemporary trumpet players. In the world of the conservatoire though, this would have been something that was competed for amongst students.

In the lesson with Nick Wright, at one point Håkan Hardenberger puts his hand on Nick's shoulder to reassure him. I never see him do this with Elizabeth, and this makes me sad and relieved at the same time.

I think back to all the men I've been taught by and my relief when they only do their job, my gratitude. I think back to the male editor and tutor twice my age who invited me to fly to Paris with him for a weekend when I was just starting out as a writer, how I laughed because I thought he was joking. How I never went to Paris, never took up his invitation to go to London to talk about my work, because I knew, of course I knew. How a young male poet could have gone to London, at least with this editor, without thinking about it, knowing that the words he heard, the invitation that was offered, was for his work.

I google Elizabeth to see if she ever made it as a trumpet player, but I can't find any trace of her online.

I'M NINETEEN and I've been booked through the college to play in a dance band. The rehearsals are unremarkable, but when we arrive at the venue for the gig, the men change into the tuxedos they've brought with them. The women are handed short lime-green snake-skin dresses with matching chokers and told to get changed.

Nobody else seems to mind. We all obey. There's not much time to get on stage.

The man who dances like Mick Jagger is also a trumpet player. We listen to Chet Baker for hours. He talks to me about tone and control of phrasing, about Chet's damaged embouchure, how he had to relearn to play again after being beaten up, but he never talks about the drinking or the drugs, his violence towards women, so I don't learn about that till much later, till I start thinking for myself.

I buy as many of Chet's albums as I can afford. He stares out from one of the covers – young and baby-faced and beautiful, his trumpet in his hand. I used to think he looked as if nothing bad had ever happened to him. Now I think he looks as if the bad things just haven't risen to the surface yet, as if the bad things are bruises that are coming into being.

I DON'T ADMIT that I love Chet's singing more than his trumpet playing, that just hearing his voice sometimes makes me cry, the imperfection of it.

Let's get lost, lost in each other's arms.

My funny Valentine. Sweet, comic Valentine.

There will never be another you.

THE MAN WHO DANCES like Mick Jagger gets his first professional job as a trumpet player on a cruise ship and travels all over the world, but for some reason, he decides not to take a mobile phone with him. There's no way of getting hold of him, and I'm hardly in when he phones. Sometimes he writes or sends a postcard. I fill my time with rehearsals, or drinking, or working behind the bar at music college.

Sometimes he phones the bar, but often I manage to miss those calls. Sometimes I'm at the far end of the room, wasting time filling up the snack machine slowly, so I don't have to do something else more onerous, or I'm in the kitchen trying to persuade the chef to make me a sandwich, and by the time I get to the phone, there's someone else waiting to use the payphone and he has to go, or his money has almost run out.

But in that long year, I am untouchable. I

move amongst the male musicians at college as if I'm made of ice, as if I might melt if they touch me with anything but brotherly love. Whilst his name is attached to mine, whilst I am waiting for him, none of them would think of doing anything, of even trying, of even asking.

When he gets back, after that long year, he goes home first to see his mum. He meets friends for a drink. By the time he makes his way to me, I know it's over, that I've waited for nothing.

Joseph Jean-Baptiste Laurent Arban was born in Lyons in 1825 and died in Paris in 1889. He was a cornetist, teacher and composer, perhaps one of the most famous and virtuosic cornet soloists of the time, although he's best remembered now for his pedagogy book, *Cornet Method* – published in 1864 and still used by brass players today.

Cornet Method is a huge tome. I still remember lugging it back and forward to music college every day. It was unthinkable to not have it with me, despite how heavy it was. The edition I have has a bright yellow cover. I find another version online that has a foreword by Arban's friend Jules Rivière. In this foreword, he talks a little about Arban's family. He was apparently one of ten brothers. His eldest brother, Louis was a balloonist. Rivière writes, 'his ascents in 1842–1843 created quite a sensation, till like most balloonists, he went up never to be heard of again'. The second brother,

Charles, invented a 'flying machine' that 'went no higher than the chimneypots', and owned a large casino and a firework factory.

Jean-Baptiste Arban went to study trumpet at the conservatoire in Paris and was instrumental in the eventual development and invention of the cornet. He wrote his own virtuosic solos, inspired and influenced by the technique and bravura of Niccolò Paganini, widely considered to be one of the greatest violinists of all time. Like Paganini, who was giving solo tours at just fifteen years old, Arban was also performing at a young age, leaving his studies at the Conservatoire de Paris aged just sixteen to tour for six months as a soloist.

Arban's arrangement of Paganini's 'Carnival of Venice' changed my life, in that all I wanted was to be able to play it, as soon as my teacher mentioned in passing that it was one of the hardest Air and Variations. I spent hours practising instead of doing other things.

Even now, after many years of not playing it, I can remember it by heart. Each variation calls for a different technique – double tonguing, triple tonguing, lyrical mastery and the flexibility to leap over octaves at speed. In the seventh variation, the notes of the theme are picked out using the lowest notes the cornet can play, and in between these notes, the cornet player must leap up and play seven semiquavers, quick as a flash, like nothing, but like a nothing that's measured, a flourish of the fingers that's perfectly in time.

It's impossible to play this variation if you have not mastered arching and flattening the tongue to change pitch. The piece itself is one of the great teachers – that the face must contain as much stillness as possible, whilst the tongue moves up and down – 'eeh' and 'aaah' inside the mouth, but none of this movement should show itself in the embouchure or the rest of the face, which should remain still, as if cast in stone.

The first time I heard this variation, it was as if there were two cornet players, one tapping out the lower notes, the other doing the technical bits in the middle, and when after a long time of trying to perfect it myself, I finally did it, heard the two cornet players alive in my body, but the sound coming from my mouth alone, I felt as if my brain had split in two, or as if my self, my doubting, fearful self had stepped aside, and my body was suddenly in charge, my fingers moving quicker than thought.

I played Arban's 'Carnival of Venice' with the music college wind band when I was an undergraduate student. I can't remember any of the rehearsals, and there's no recording of the event. It only exists now in my mind, and perhaps, if I'm lucky, the minds of some of the other people that were there. I'm under no illusion that the performance was worthy of mention anywhere apart from here. Still, it's enough to know that once I stood on stage and played it, that I did not miss a variation out, that I did not falter, or if I did, it was a small enough misstep to keep going until the end.

Niccolò Paganini developed extended techniques such as ricochet bowing, flying staccatos and left-hand pizzicato on the violin, travelling across Europe to give performances. Arban, following in his footsteps, is said to have been the first brass player to use triple tonguing – his ambition was to elevate the cornet to the same status as classical instruments such as the flute or violin.

In Arban's introduction to his *Cornet Method*, he says that triple tonguing should be produced by the use of the tongue striking out the syllables 'tu tu ku', so the last of the three notes is produced by the back of the tongue against the throat. This enables the player to perform passages at great speed that would not be possible when just using single tonguing.

The teacher who taught me triple tonguing advised me to use 'du gu du'. I guess the reasoning behind the change in syllables is that the du and the gu are easier to produce than the sharper sounds of tu and ku, but I'm not sure why he changed the order so that the softer syllable was in the middle. I never asked, and it was never explained. I haven't been able to unlearn this way of tonguing, although I've tried. None of my teachers that came after ever noticed I was not using the recognised pattern, and once I realised, I worked hard to disguise my adaptation.

Paganini's virtuosity was rumoured to be part of his reward for a pact with the devil. Audience members swore they'd seen the devil helping him play during concerts. It's thought now that he may have had Marfan's syndrome, a rare genetic condition characterised by unusually long and slender limbs, fingers and toes. This could explain the ability of Paganini to play over three octaves, something considered physically impossible by most violinists today.

Apparently, Paganini embraced the rumours of his friendship with the devil, often arriving at concerts in a black coach, drawn by four black horses, and dressed completely in black. Still, I wonder what other reaction was left to him, other than to embrace it, to exaggerate the performance of it. Karl Knights, in his essay 'The Face Not Seen', first published in *The Dark Horse*, argues that the link between disability and evil – whether this was disability as representation of evil or just association with it – 'has its roots in the medieval notion that bodily difference was a manifestation of past sin'.

Paganini once said, 'I am not handsome, but when women hear me play, they come crawling to my feet.' I think I would have been one of those women – when I was fourteen, I had a huge and unexplainable crush on the middle-aged Principal Cornet player of the senior brass band. We were all offered lessons with a member of the senior band, and imagine my delight when I was told I would be receiving a cornet lesson from A, the Principal Cornet Player.

My only ambition in life at this point was to be good enough to join the senior band and work my way up through the third cornet section, and then the second cornet section, until eventually I made it to the front row, to finally sit next to A, where he would fall madly in love with me. My dreams were hazy after this point in my imagined future as to what would happen next, but I was sure the lesson was the first step towards my dream.

During the lesson, which took place in the bandroom in an upstairs room, he asked me to play a duet with him. I fainted shortly after taking my cornet from the case, probably from over-excitement. My dad came and carried me down the stairs. I think he knew why I'd fainted, but pretended that he didn't.

Paganini had a son called Achille Paganini. He accompanied his father on tours and cared for him in later years when Paganini became unable to speak, pressing his ear to his father's mouth and acting as an interpreter.

Jules Rivière mentions in his foreword that Arban had a daughter. He says Arban left everything to her, although Rivière doesn't name her, and now I can't find any information about her online. I have no idea if she also played music, if she was a cornet player, what she did when he went travelling across the world, who looked after her, who put her to bed, fed her, dressed her, how old was she when he died, did she dance when he played the 'Carnival of Venice', his 'Fantasie Brilliante', his 'Fantasie and Variations on Actaeon'?

I'm twenty-one and have just finished music college. I've been offered a gig playing trumpet with an amateur dance band who are going on tour to Germany. They need a lead trumpet player. Whilst it's not paid, it's a free holiday, I tell myself. It's experience, and one thing can lead unexpectedly to another.

I get the train down to Devon and I'm met at the station by the conductor and his wife. I can tell they're not sure of me. They don't know if I'm up to the job. Later, they tell me I didn't look like a trumpet player.

The next day we set off in a coach for Germany. I don't know that this trip will change my life, that I'll meet someone who will nearly break me, who will stop me seeing my friends, who will stop me.

He stopped me for the longest time.

For the shortest time really – only a year, and in the grand scheme of things, a year is not a long time. And yet, it stretches over my life – it casts a shadow that wanes and rises. You could say the trumpet took me to him.

AND YET, I'M HAPPY in that week, before I really knew him. I'm staying with a host family, along with the bass player from the band, who is a few years older than me and embroiled in an unhappy and protracted affair with a married man back in England.

We get drunk every night at the local pub with the daughter of our host family. She brings her bicycle to the pub, and on the way home, we manage to fit all three of us on it, one standing on the pedals, one on the seat, one on the handlebars. We're weaving all over the road, and above us, shooting stars are falling. Somehow, I know that this night will be a tiny light inside me, that I will carry it with me into the future.

IN THE MISSING YEAR, the lost year, I live with the man I met in Germany and he slowly unravels me. By the end of the year, I am just one single thread, spun out, undone. I am almost nothing.

During this year, I train to be a secondary school music teacher, specialising in peripatetic teaching. I teach Year 7 *Rhythm and Pulse* and tell nobody that when I'm with the man I met in Germany, I keep my eyes on the floor, so he can't accuse me of anything, like flirting, or looking at another man or looking at anybody.

I teach Year 8 *The Blues* and I don't tell anyone that I feel as if my life is a film, but I'm watching it from the outside, and someone else has control of my limbs, my arms, someone else is moving my body for me.

I teach Year 9 *Film Music* but nobody knows about the nights I don't sleep, that sometimes he does not let me close my eyes, that I alternate between crying and staring into space until morning.

As part of my training, I travel around with a trombone teacher from Birmingham Music Service. He's kind and generous and really it's because of him that I qualify at all, because of those days away from the classroom. I don't tell the man I met in Germany that I spend two days a week in a car, alone with another man. I'm afraid of what he might do if he learns this, what he might demand I do.

Once upon a time a ghost lived in the middle of a city, in a tall tower that reached up to the sky. A lord lived in the tower with the ghost, and though the lord left the shining keys of the tower out on full display, glittering in the moonlight, or turning warm under the sun, the ghost never dared to reach out her hand and touch them, never mind use them to open a door.

The ghost owned a silver trumpet wreathed in gold. The trumpet was made to fit only the hand of the ghost, and was only ever supposed to be played by her. One day the lord took the silver trumpet away, though he knew it was the most precious thing she owned.

The lord climbed to the top of the tower and dangled the trumpet over the edge and shouted into the wind. He described how it would shatter into a million pieces when it met the ground many leagues below. The ghost felt as if it was not the trumpet in his hand, but her body being held out to the sky, her body in his grip with no hope of escape.

And it was in that moment of despair, before the lord grew tired of the game he played, that she remembered who she was, that she was not of this world and so not born to be owned, that though this world was of his making, that meant that she could slip from it when she chose, that there was no tower, no man's hand that could hold her, that neither keys nor walls held dominion over her.

When she realised all of this, she waited until the lord left to visit another kingdom with another tower that he'd built by hand. Then she took back the silver trumpet and passed through the bones of the tower and went far, far away, leaving no trace of herself behind.

Many years later, the ghost had occasion to reach inside herself, and found that she was haunted by the ghost of the tower itself, that she must have put it there for safe keeping, so it could never creep up on her again and swallow her whole. She plucked out the tower and stood it on her silvery palm, and although she could have crushed it then, or folded it smaller and smaller, or broken it down into its constituent parts, she found she was not ready to do this. Perhaps she would never be ready. Call it a folly then, she thought, placing it back in her chest.

After I escape the man I met in Germany, the man I lived with for a year, I make an appointment to see a doctor. The doctor has long, brown, wavy hair. I make the appointment because I've become suddenly, inexplicably, deaf in one ear. Or maybe I'm remembering it wrong. Is it possible I'm making it up – this memory I have of hearing voices and cars and music as if I'm under water, or as if I'm listening through one of those shells that hold the sound of the ocean inside?

She looks in my ear and tells me it's an ear infection and writes out a prescription. She asks if everything else is okay and I find myself telling her about the man I met in Germany, about the year I spent with him, about not lifting my eyes, about bruises, and spitting, and sleepless nights and being trapped and lost and giving in, about always giving in.

I'd like to tell her now that she probably,

almost certainly saved me, but I don't know her name, can't remember the address of the surgery, or even the part of the city it was in.

She says that all of this, all of this that has happened to me, that was done to me has a name. She gives me a helpline to ring, but the number is always engaged.

AFTER I LEAVE the man I met in Germany, I get a job at the other end of the country as a peripatetic brass teacher for Cumbria Music Service. My teaching area ranges from Barrow to Millom, up to Kendal and Appleby and Kirby Stephen, but shortly before I'm due to start, I fail my driving test, the one thing the job offer was conditional on.

My dad pays on his credit card for an intense weekend course so I can get a provisional license to drive a scooter. The teacher is an ex-Hells Angel, and on the first day, he walks backwards across the car park in front of me, arms open wide. I wobble towards him on a borrowed scooter as he shouts 'Come on. Come on, darling. That's it. Come on.' I feel both humiliated and loved when he calls me darling.

I'M IN THE FIRST WEEK of my full-time teaching job for Cumbria Music Service and I've been sent to a teaching conference for newly qualified teachers. I'm deathly bored. All through lunch and dinner all the other teachers do is talk about teaching.

In the final session, as I'm preparing to become even more fed-up, a speaker stands up and asks the audience to think about their 'magic weavers' – the teachers who made a difference to them as students.

I've never heard of this term before, and find it slightly cheesy. The speaker then comes off script and says that her magic weaver is in the audience – that she hasn't seen her for years, since she was a girl, but that she wanted to tell her what an impact she made. She asks us all to get in touch with our own magic weavers and tell them, before it's too late.

By this point, I'm in tears. All of my irritated cynicism and indifference and boredom with constant talk about teaching has vanished. All I can think about are the wonderful teachers I've known – my history teacher, Mr C, who was so strict I was terrified of him, but who I wanted so much to impress. My English teacher, Mrs S, who I used to give poems and stories to that I'd written outside of class. She would always read them, and write comments in the margins so it felt as if I was having a private conversation with her. My music teachers and trumpet teachers and band conductors. I'd never told any of them what a difference they made to me.

When I get to Cumbria, I drive around on my scooter with my music books in the hat box and my trumpet strapped to my back, all through the autumn term. I think I'm going to have students like me, who will want to go to music college, who will practise every day. The reality is very different. I have students who practise a little bit. After a few months, I can tell if they've practised once during the week or twice. I have students who take up the trumpet because they enjoy the half-hour respite from 'proper' lessons. I have a private student who tells me the best bit about her lesson is seeing my rather overweight ginger and white cat, who sits on her knee whilst she plays. I have students who are talented enough to get to music college but are just not interested. I have a student who only needs to hear something once and she can play it but refuses to learn to read music. I have a trombone student I keep one step ahead of, until

he reaches Grade 5, and then I hand him over, with relief, to another teacher.

I spend my weeks telling children not to hit their mouthpieces with the palm of their hand, even though it makes a satisfying sound. I tell them to breathe as if their bodies are balloons that they must fill up with air. I tell them that what they put in comes out. We have long note competitions. I repeat myself often. I do not understand why I sit outside each school and have to gather myself before I go in.

A SILVER TRUMPET, wrapped in reeds.
No. Try again.

A silver trumpet, embellished in gold and wrapped in reeds.
No. Try again.

A silver trumpet, found in the south-east corner of the tomb. Wrapped in reeds.
No. Try again.

A silver trumpet, lying under a calcite lamp. Wrapped in reeds. The south-east corner of the tomb.
No. Try again.

A silver trumpet, engraved with a whorl of sepals and calices to represent the lotus flower. Embellished in gold. Wrapped in reeds. The south-east

corner of the tomb. The calcite lamp.
No.

A silver trumpet. Wrapped in reeds. Inside the trumpet a wooden core, to prevent it being squashed.
No.

A silver trumpet, found with a red pottery stopper with blue decoration, the ribs of an ox, a broken wooden label with no inscription, a fragment of pot containing a black substance.
Almost.

From 'Tutankhamun: The Anatomy of an Excavation',
Note Card 175, The Howard Carter Archives,
The Griffin Institute

One of the first friends I make in Cumbria is a guitar teacher called B, who is a little older than me and also works for Cumbria Music Service.

B lives in the same town and is quiet and gentle. My scooter keeps breaking down and he comes and picks me up and gives me a lift home. He shows me around, invites me to his house to meet his friends and his girlfriend. I can tell he worries about me. I don't tell him about the lost year, but I think he knows I'm lost. I briefly go out with one of his friends, but it doesn't last. B doesn't hold that against me either. He's unfailingly kind and I'm suspicious at first.

I only know B for a few months before he dies in a car crash, on the way home from work. He has an asthma attack whilst driving and loses control on the A590, on a part of the road that flicks back and forward.

The trees keep the road in shadow throughout summer and winter. I never drive that road without thinking of him.

It's not till I become a teacher that I learn I don't understand vibrato, or more accurately, I don't know how to put into words how to produce vibrato, or how to make it stop. I try to explain it to a pupil. I play a phrase from 'Cavatina', close my eyes, and I'm back there again, in the band room. I'm trying to sing without my voice, I'm trying to yearn without knowing what I'm missing. I know this is not a good enough explanation.

Wikipedia helpfully tells me that there are three types of vibrato – a hand vibrato, a lip or jaw vibrato and a diaphragm or air vibrato, but none of these quite fit, none of them seem quite right for what I'm doing.

On the website *The Brass Band Portal*, there's a post from 2001 by someone called Dave Buckley, where he recounts a lesson given by Alain Trudel, one of the world's best trombone players. Buckley writes that when Trudel was asked about the production of vibrato, he 'looked quite mystified and then replied "You just do what is correct for the music"'. Dave Buckley continues, 'In other words if you want the sound warmed up tell your body and let it happen in whatever way sounds best – don't over intellectualise it.'

If you grew up in a brass band, you are soaked in vibrato – everybody uses it – a shimmering, living sound. It's something that settles inside you, as if it's a bird, and you are a tree it's chosen to live in. And this is not a satisfactory explanation either. My pupil asks – yes, but how do you do it? And I say, I think it into existence. And then I imagine it away.

I'm playing in a performance of Handel's *Messiah* in St Bees. It's an hour and forty minutes' drive from Barrow, and I'm nervous about the journey back in the dark on my own. The most direct route is over Corney Fell, a road that's regularly closed in bad weather. I've only just passed my driving license, only just moved from scooter to car. B says he'll come over, listen to the concert, and drive back so I can follow on behind.

In the interval, I notice I've had multiple missed calls from B's girlfriend. She rings again, as I'm standing there with my phone in my hand, looking at the screen. I answer the phone and she tells me that B is dead. I'm confused. I think she's made some terrible mistake, and I even say that, with something almost like anger in my voice. *No, you're wrong. You must be mistaken.* Later, I find it hard to forgive myself for this, even though I know it was the shock, because until then I'd been lucky, not to know anyone young who was so present in the world and then ripped out of it so quickly.

When I put the phone down, I go outside and lean my forehead on the wall of the church. I feel as if I can't breathe, as if I'm going to have a panic attack. Then I have one of the strangest experiences of my life. My head is still resting on the wall of the church. The stone is cool against my skin. Suddenly, I feel a wave of calm wash through me, but it's as if this calm is coming from the wall of the church.

I know if I stop touching the church wall with my forehead it will stop, and I don't want it to. It's the only thing keeping me here, the only thing stopping other terrible, thoughtless, angry words bursting from my mouth. The interval finishes. The people smoking move back inside the church, and I follow.

There's still the third part of the *Messiah* to play. If the first part of the *Messiah* concerns itself with redemption, and the second with suffering, the third is all about victory over death.

I wasn't thinking about any of this at the time, but I've thought about it since then. All through the rest of that night, I kept looking towards the back of the hall, expecting to see B standing there, covered in rain and slightly flustered from being late.

*The trumpet shall sound
and the dead shall be raised
the dead shall be raised incorruptible*

But he was not raised, he did not come back, and now I rarely say his name.

I RUN MY OWN junior brass band now, and I arrange a trip to take them to an orchestral concert. I can still see the disgust on my A-Level teacher's face when I admitted I'd never been to listen to an orchestra. I'm determined these kids will hear one. We hire a coach. The nearest professional orchestral concert taking place this year is in Lancaster, over an hour and a half away.

One ten-year-old girl keeps saying we're going to London. I correct her, and say we're going to Lancaster. She shrugs. 'Same difference.' Later on, her class teacher tells me she's never left Barrow, or even been in a car as her parents don't drive. This seems incredible to me, too incredible to be true, but her excitement at being on the coach is real.

On the way to the concert, I stand up in the aisle to give the usual lecture – don't wander off, look both ways before crossing the road. I feel something wet hit my leg. At first I think one of the children has squirted me with water. It's worse than that though – a boy has thrown up and it's all over my trousers.

At the concert, complete with damp legs and suffering from the indignity of a wet paper towel mop-up, I settle down in my chair as the orchestra tunes up. As the last concert A dies away, my kids start clapping. My heart cracks open a little, and I curse myself for not explaining that this is not the first piece, for not remembering how strange these rituals are if you've never experienced them before.

I remember to tell them not to clap between movements, or at least I tell the child sitting next to me and he passes the message down the row.

It's my first term delivering Wider Opportunities. Instead of small group and individual lessons, I'll now primarily be delivering whole-class tuition, to fulfil the stated aim of the government for every child at primary school to learn an instrument for free for at least one year. I think it's going to be awful, that the children will pick up bad habits, that it will not produce any players of worth.

My first Wider Opportunities lesson is a disaster. The instruments – ten trumpets, ten cornets and ten baritones – arrive from the central office with minutes to spare before the lesson actually starts. When I open the first case, I am thankful there are no students in the room to hear my cursing. Every single instrument is in pieces. The valves have been placed into a plastic bag. Each one will need putting in the right way and oiling. The slides are in another clear plastic bag. They will all need to be greased before being put together.

WIDER OPPORTUNITIES gets better after that first awful lesson when the instruments arrived in pieces. It's a disciplined way of teaching and I find no difference in the way the children learn in these large groups than in the smaller groups I used to teach. I encourage teachers and teaching assistants to learn alongside their class, and the most successful classes are the ones where the teaching staff are involved as well.

Schools are entitled to one year of free tuition. They can then buy in more years of Wider Opportunities if they want to, and many do, using the lesson as a cheap cover for PPA (planning, preparation and assessment) for their class teacher. For the schools that don't, the children with parents who can afford to pay for lessons and instrument hire carry on – the rest lose the opportunity, which I find deeply frustrating.

I start to arrange concerts with the junior

band to fundraise for children who want to continue learning. They come to rehearsal every Monday at 6pm. Tuition is free, uniform is free, but most importantly the instruments are free.

A child runs ahead to fling open the door to the music room, but recoils from the handle, which is encrusted with bogies, like the smallest green stalactites in the world.

I'm team-teaching with a violin teacher in the early days of whole class instrumental tuition. The Year 3 class are sitting with their violins, but one girl is slowly plucking the violin bow, peeling each horse hair delicately from tip to tip. The violin teacher rushes over, snatches the bow away and says 'Now you'll just have to pluck it instead'. Because the violin teacher is one of the gentlest people I know, she manages to control her exasperation, apart from when she says the word 'pluck'. When she says 'pluck', it's as if the word is the hardest pebble in the world and has rolled on the floor between us. The girl is oblivious, or maybe still in the sway of the extreme satisfaction of peeling a violin bow. Maybe it's like peeling glue from your hand in infant school, or biting the skin around your fingernails. Maybe it feels that good.

I SPEND A YEAR teaching the recorder. I have to learn alongside the children. I can't remember anything from childhood. I lecture the class of Year 3s so much about how terrible recorders sound when overblown, that by the time I let them have a go, it comes out as the tiniest pip. The following week, feeling guilty, I teach them the note 'A' to add to the note 'B' that we did last week, but half of them keep forgetting to cover the second hole of the recorder. The clash of the two notes is awful. I shout in desperation, 'Cover your A-holes!'

Every year my sister and I take part in a local music festival, conducting our brass bands. This year I have three brass bands at the festival – my sister has two. Mine are all based in Barrow: Barrow Shipyard Junior Band, made up of players from both primary and secondary schools; a local primary school band where the whole of Key Stage 3 plays brass; and finally Brasstastic, made up of primary school children from across Barrow. My sister's band is Egremont Junior Band and a school band from the west coast of Cumbria. The adjudicator stands up to give his results. The hall is full of parents and children. He asks anyone who has been taught by myself or my twin sister to stand up. It feels like the whole room stands – hundreds of children, although I don't know the number now, have no way of knowing. I don't feel proud very often, or for very long, but I did in that moment.

Greengates and Yarlside and Lindal and Marton.

St Pius and Ormsgill and Dowdales and Roose.

Ireleth St Peters and Furness Academy.

South Walney, Holy Family and Dalton St Marys.

Dane Ghyll and St Pauls and Our Lady of the Rosary.

Monday comes, Monday comes, start all over again.

SOMETIMES I ARRIVE at school and the children are out on a trip, or rehearsing for a play, or doing extra maths, extra PE, a knitting lesson, they're out at Forest Schools, they're changing their library book or waiting to see the headteacher, they're in an important assembly or helping the caretaker, they've forgotten their instruments or they've forgotten their mouthpieces, the teacher has to listen to them read, or they have to finish their handwriting practice, or they're still eating their lunch, or the dinner ladies have them lined up against the wall for bad behaviour or they have to tidy up the paints; and sometimes the receptionist forgets to tell me any of this and I sit in the classroom and wait for ten minutes before going to try and find the missing children, searching down corridors and knocking on classroom doors, the teacher looking relieved or irritated or happy at the interruption; and sometimes the receptionist will remember to tell me as I walk through the door, before I even sign in; and at some schools the receptionist will ring me as I pull up in the car park, before I unload the bag of music books, the spare trumpet, the spare baritone, the spare mouthpieces, my trumpet, my laptop; sometimes they ring as I'm sat there, willing myself to get out of my car and they tell me I'm not needed and it's these receptionists that I am most grateful for and I say oh what a shame and oh well there's always next week and I get back into my car and pull out my pen and notebook and wind all the windows up and I put the heater on full blast no matter the temperature outside and I begin, of course I begin to write.

Shortly after moving to Cumbria, I join a monthly poetry group. The group meet upstairs in a pub in Ulverston, a town about eight miles away from where I live. It feels fantastical to me that I can walk past people drinking in the bar and go upstairs to a room where people are sitting around a table and talking about poetry. It feels like another world, hidden beneath the surface of the world I thought I lived in.

INSIDE THE BALTIC Centre for Contemporary Art in Newcastle, Cornelia Parker's sculpture, *Doubtful Sounds*, is being exhibited. It consists of sixty silver-plated brass instruments, suspended from the ceiling with stainless steel wires and lit by a single lightbulb. Every instrument has been flattened. It feels like a room full of ghosts, silver apparitions that gently turn on their wires, as if they're now so insubstantial they will move in the slightest breeze.

It's the first time I've walked into an art gallery and been moved, the first time I've felt art looking back at me. I think it's the most beautiful thing I've ever seen. Brass instruments like pressed flowers in the open book of a room. It's shocking how utterly themselves they are, despite having the breath taken from them, despite not being able to do what they were born to do.

Another of Cornelia Parker's sculptures containing crushed brass instruments is *Breathless*. It has 54 brass band instruments and is currently exhibited at the V&A in London. This sculpture is also suspended, but between two floors of the V&A, so you can see it in two ways, both from above and below. The instruments are horizontal rather than vertical. I haven't seen this one in person, but the images I find online feel much more static to me, maybe because the instruments are taking the place of both a floor and a ceiling, or maybe it's because it looks as if they've just been taken out of their cases and left there, abandoned.

This sculpture caused a lot of controversy at the time, with Norman Harvey of the Churchill Society calling it an 'act of vandalism and an absolute scandal'. The artist defended her work, arguing that the instruments were defunct ones that would have been scrapped anyway.

In the description online at the V&A, it says that the work is an 'attempt by the artist to explore such ideas of duality as silence/noise, upper class/lower class and death/resurrection'. Apart from being beautiful to look at, for me *Breathless* asks questions about the past and future of brass bands. If the past of brass bands is rooted in the pits and collieries, the shipyards and steelworks, where does their future lie?

I'm playing in the *Messiah* again, in St Bees again, this time a memorial concert for the victims of Derrick Bird, who killed thirteen people (including himself) and injured eleven others in June 2010. Most of the victims were picked seemingly at random – people that Bird drove past who were walking their dogs or riding their bikes or gardening, or people that he beckoned over, who maybe thought he was just asking for directions.

I'm told that the twin sister of one of the people who died is singing in the choir behind me. There's something about the singing and this terrible loss, and how neither can completely swallow or cover the other. And of course, every time I play in the *Messiah*, I think of B, imagine him standing at the back of the church. I wonder if we would still be friends if he'd lived, or would life have made us drift apart by now?

The day of the shootings, my twin sister

sheltered upstairs in her house in Frizington with two students who'd just arrived for a lesson. Their mother rang from the newsagent down the road and told her to lock the doors and take the boys and stay upstairs. If my sister had dared to look out of the window, she'd have seen the gunman pass by once, twice in his car.

Behold, I show you a mystery.
We shall not all sleep, but we shall all be changed.
In a moment, in the twinkling of an eye
at the last trumpet.

IN LESSON AFTER LESSON, I'm asked by students what the difference is between the trumpet and the cornet. I'm always rushing and there's never enough time to do everything, to teach whatever I'm teaching that week, to fill in the practice diary, to be encouraging, to be interested, to answer questions. I always mumble something about the cornet being smaller, more compact. I know this is not a useful or complete answer to the question.

Now I look back and feel guilty that I didn't try harder to answer, that I wasn't a better teacher, that I didn't use it as an opportunity to encourage the students to research and find out for themselves.

I could have told them about the history of the instruments, that the trumpet was made to stand out, to play fanfares and at ceremonial occasions, that the cornet was designed to blend in, part of a larger cornet section in a brass band, that understanding this is central to understanding the difference between them.

I could have told the student that both instruments are exactly the same length of tubing, but the cornet has four curves whilst the trumpet has two. I could have talked about the 'shepherd's crook' shape to the cornet, how the extra curves make it look smaller, how a cornet is less likely to 'droop' when given to a young player.

I could have talked about the trumpet's cylindrical bore and the cornet's conical one, how the bell flare on each instrument happens in a different place. That the bell of the trumpet is further from the mouth, meaning the cornet feels closer to the heart, meaning the trumpet is better for hiding behind, meaning, meaning, meaning – what?

I could have kept it simple, saying the cornet sound is mellow and rich, the trumpet sound bright and piercing, but that is so over-simplistic I can hardly bear to write it, and I know it's not quite true, because I've heard trumpet players who pick up a cornet and still sound like trumpet players, and cornet players who pick up a trumpet and sound only like cornet players, and this is a mystery to me and also perfectly clear.

I could have talked to them about cornets being part of a working-class tradition of brass banding, that at one time nearly every pit and colliery and shipyard would have had a brass band attached to them, that it was a way of keeping workers from organising politically and causing trouble. But that might have led to a discussion about class and I definitely wouldn't have had time for that in a thirty-minute lesson.

I could have said – I was given a cornet for free, and I worked and saved and scrimped for my trumpet.

I could have said – when I played the cornet, I was a big fish in a small pond. When I played the trumpet, I drowned.

I could have said – I have earned money with my trumpet, but nothing with my cornet.

I could have said – when I auditioned for music college on the trumpet, I was asked again and again why I didn't just come with my cornet, because they could tell I was a cornet player.

But though these are answers, they're not

the answers to this question. How alarming that even from this distance, after all these years, I'm floundering when I try to begin, that there's still an impossibility here when I try to articulate the difference in language.

I stop performing. It's become endlessly painful for me. I can't stop worrying that I'm not good enough, that I'm out of tune. It happens gradually at first. I practise less and less, and then one week I realise I haven't picked up the trumpet at all, and haven't missed it.

It coincides with starting to take poetry more seriously, as if language has flowed into the space the trumpet used to take up. The dizzying freedom of just being able to delete a bad line, or even a bad poem. Criticism clearly directed toward the poem, rather than me. The comparison to how criticism feels as a trumpet player, how it settles in my body.

The poem as a tiny shield, defending the musician part of me that needs protecting.

AT THE MONTHLY poetry group, someone leaves a pamphlet on the table, advertising residential writing courses at Tŷ Newydd, the National Writing Centre in Wales. I decide to book on a course. I'm nervous about going, so nervous I get completely lost on the way there and have a panic attack in the car. By the time I arrive, I'm an hour late. I seriously consider turning around and just driving back home, but somehow force myself to go in.

The tutors are Nigel Jenkins and Sarah Kennedy. Sarah's work astonishes me in its capacity to hold pain and violence, and yet to turn these experiences into art, into an object that feels as real as a painting, a made thing. In a tutorial with Nigel Jenkins, he tells me to approach my writing in the same way as I've approached trumpet playing – to read every day, and write every day, and if I do these things, I'll be published within a year.

It's my first summer of not playing the trumpet, the first time since the age of ten of not practising every day. There's a great sadness inside me, but also a relief, as if a hand on the back of my neck has been removed. To meet a poet at this point, and for them to use that metaphor, that writing can be like trumpet playing, that one can take the place of the other, that I can approach poetry with the same discipline, the same rigour I'd been trained to use as a musician, but which was now idling inside me, to be told that writing is something I can work hard at, that reading, which I've always loved, was intertwined and necessary and vital, these words, that course, these tutors, that place – all of it changed my life.

It's 2016, and I apply to do a PhD at Manchester Metropolitan University. I'm offered a Vice Chancellor's Bursary, and I finally leave music teaching for good, after years of gradually reducing my hours.

During those years as a part-time music teacher, I've been working as a writer, running workshops and residential courses, taking on residencies when I could fit it around my job, performing at festivals and reading series across the UK and Europe. My plan is to continue to work as a writer whilst studying for the PhD.

I miss conducting the band, though this is all I miss about my former life, my other life. I miss teaching them something, about counting, about tuning, about listening, and the sudden ghostly feeling of my teacher, and my teacher's teacher speaking through me.

My conductor R used to say *nobody is bigger than the band*. He said this when he was cross with someone – for leaving to join another band, or thinking of leaving, or if their attendance at rehearsal was patchy. I believed in it – that a brass band is a living, breathing creature in and of itself, that as long as there are two people left, the band will live on and somehow survive.

But I also think that the great strength and weakness of a brass band, more so than any other ensemble, is its reliance on the conductor to hold it together. It's not that the conductor is bigger than the band – without the band there would be no conductor – but more that the conductor is a magnet that draws the band to them.

I left my junior brass band behind when I left teaching. I thought it would survive – that I was doing the right thing – making a clean break. The band had around thirty-five children taking part and maybe five parents who were also learning to play an instrument alongside their children. It folded a couple of years after I left, and this still both angers and upsets me.

I should have kept better records, I should have recorded them playing together more, I should have taken more photographs.

The kids who came early to set out the chairs and put the drum kit together and assemble the music stands. The teenagers who looked after the new children and would point out their place if they got lost in the music. The ones who would always, always forget something – part of their uniform, or their instrument, or their mouthpiece.

We had a whole library of film music and pop music and pieces I thought they'd love – but one of their favourite pieces for years and years was Pachelbel's 'Canon'. It was always impossible to predict what they'd like, what they'd never get bored of playing.

The conductor of a band needs to love the band. They need to tell themselves nobody is bigger than the band and they must mean themselves as well as their best player, because if they don't believe the band will live on without them, then what's the point of any of it?

Imagine being there, in the Cairo museum for the BBC recording. The oldest trumpet in the world is about to be played. Just before broadcasting, there is a power cut. They go live in flickering candlelight.

I HARDLY PLAY FOR YEARS until eventually I join a ten-piece soul band. We play long hot gigs in working-men's clubs, at weddings, in nightclubs. The dancefloor is full of bodies writhing and twisting. I have a microphone clipped to the bell of my trumpet. The band is held together by the drummer. There's no conductor, nobody to watch, other than the in-breath of the singers, other than the lifting of the sticks by the drummer from the corner of my eye.

One night I faint on stage, which reminds me of another time of very public fainting. On that occasion I was marching around Pontefract Race Course in the summer of 2003 with the ex-army band, hungover and dehydrated. Both times, it's as if a black curtain falls over my eyes.

Every November, I play the Last Post in my back garden. I don't know if anybody's listening.

John Donne wrote, 'At the round earth's imagined corners, blow/Your trumpets, angels: and arise, arise/from death, you numberless infinities/of souls, and to your scattered bodies go'.

I love the twisting of the line here, how it's impossible to stop once you start. I thought Donne was saying that it's the trumpets that will call the souls back into their scattered bodies, but now, reading it again, I think the trumpet is only the signal – it's language that calls the spirit to find the body it belongs to. The angels blow their trumpets, and then Donne himself tells the soul to 'arise, arise/from death'.

I pick the trumpet up in my left hand. It still feels like it fits there, though I haven't played for months now. This instrument is twenty-two years old and has been with me over half my life.

The lacquer is worn away in multiple places, especially around the valve casing. The worst place is at the front of the first valve, where my left thumb often slides from the first valve ring and up onto the casing when I'm playing in the higher register, but the lacquer's eroding everywhere.

Human sweat has acid in it, and it's this that eats away at the lacquer on brass instruments. I don't remember who told me, maybe one of the male trumpet players at music college, carefully wiping down their trumpet with a bar towel they carried in their cases after every rehearsal.

I've never wiped my trumpet down after playing. Maybe I haven't looked after it enough, but I never had any interest in it looking pristine.

If someone else picks it up, I want them to feel the marks my hands have made on the metal. I don't want to wipe the sweat, the work away.

There's one dent in the trumpet on the second valve slide. The dent is smaller than my fingernail, and I can't remember how it got there. All of the slides still move. The valves still go up and down smoothly.

If you held my trumpet up in front of your face, but pointing the bell toward the sky, you might notice something else a little odd. The main tube that leads to the bell is bent slightly to the right. It doesn't run in a straight parallel line alongside the leadpipe as it should. This is the legacy of a car crash from about ten years ago when a transit van ploughed into the back of me. I thought the trumpet – stored in the boot in a soft leather gig bag – would be a write-off, but it was repaired, resurrected from being squashed and almost split in half.

So this trumpet has survived a car crash and multiple house moves across the country, and my laziness at never wiping it down, and in all honesty, not cleaning it enough, never giving it enough baths, enough attention, enough love, because yes, you should bathe a trumpet, you should strip it down to its constituent parts, taking out the valves first and laying them on a towel, taking out the first valve slide and the second valve slide and the third valve slide and the main tuning slide, letting them sink to the bottom of the bath of water and soak; you should push a bendy brush through the trumpet as many different ways as you can find to clean out the hidden places it contains, clean out all that your breath has deposited inside it. I should have done this much more often than I have.

I curve my right hand into the letter 'C', place my fingertips on the valves, my little finger in the finger ring. I take a deep breath. I ask what I have always asked of it, and we begin.

Acknowledgements

Thank you to Ann and Peter Sansom – for your friendship over the years, and your enthusiasm and support for this project.

Thank you to Katie at The Poetry Business for her careful and thorough attention, and endless patience in the production process for this book.

Thank you to Emma Burleigh for the wonderful illustrations.

Thank you to Arts Council England for a Developing Your Creative Practice Grant. Part of the grant was used to buy time to write and expand what was a short essay into a full book.

Thank you to all of the bands that I have played with over the years for providing much of the inspiration, love and friendship that this book has been built on – including, but not limited to Unity Brass Band, Unity Brass Junior Band, The Yorkshire Volunteers, Leeds

College of Music Big Band, Leeds College of Music Symphony Orchestra, Leeds College of Music New Music Ensemble, Big Jesse and his Fancy Band, Sisters of Swing, Furness Music Centre, Cumbria Brass Ensemble, Barrow Shipyard Band, Barrow Shipyard Junior Band, Brasstastic, St Pius Brass Band, Askam Brass Band and my beloved Soul Survivors, who reignited my love of playing, after it had lain dormant for so long.

Thank you to Helen Wedgwood – you were the best teaching assistant I could ask for!

Thank you to the teachers and conductors I've met along the way especially Rob Boulter, my band conductor and Paul Bennett, my trumpet teacher, who taught me not only about trumpet playing, but also about teaching, and how to live a creative life.

Thank you to my dear friend and trumpet player Dave Boraston. I hope we know each other for another twenty years, and another twenty.

Thank you to my mum and dad, who made it possible

for me to play music in the first place, and who have always encouraged and supported me. When I put the trumpet down and didn't want to play anymore, you told me it would always be there for me, and I didn't believe you at the time. You were right.

Thank you to my husband Chris and my daughter Ally. Your patience and support not only whilst I'm writing, but also while I've been getting 'back into practice' means everything to me.

Finally, thank you to my sister Jody. At the time when we played together for all of those years, I didn't realise what a wonderful thing it is to play in a band with your family. I hope we can do it again soon.